My name is _______________________.

A a
Apple
A A A A A A
A A A A A
a a a a a
a a a a a

B b
Book
B
b

1
1
Cake

Dolphin

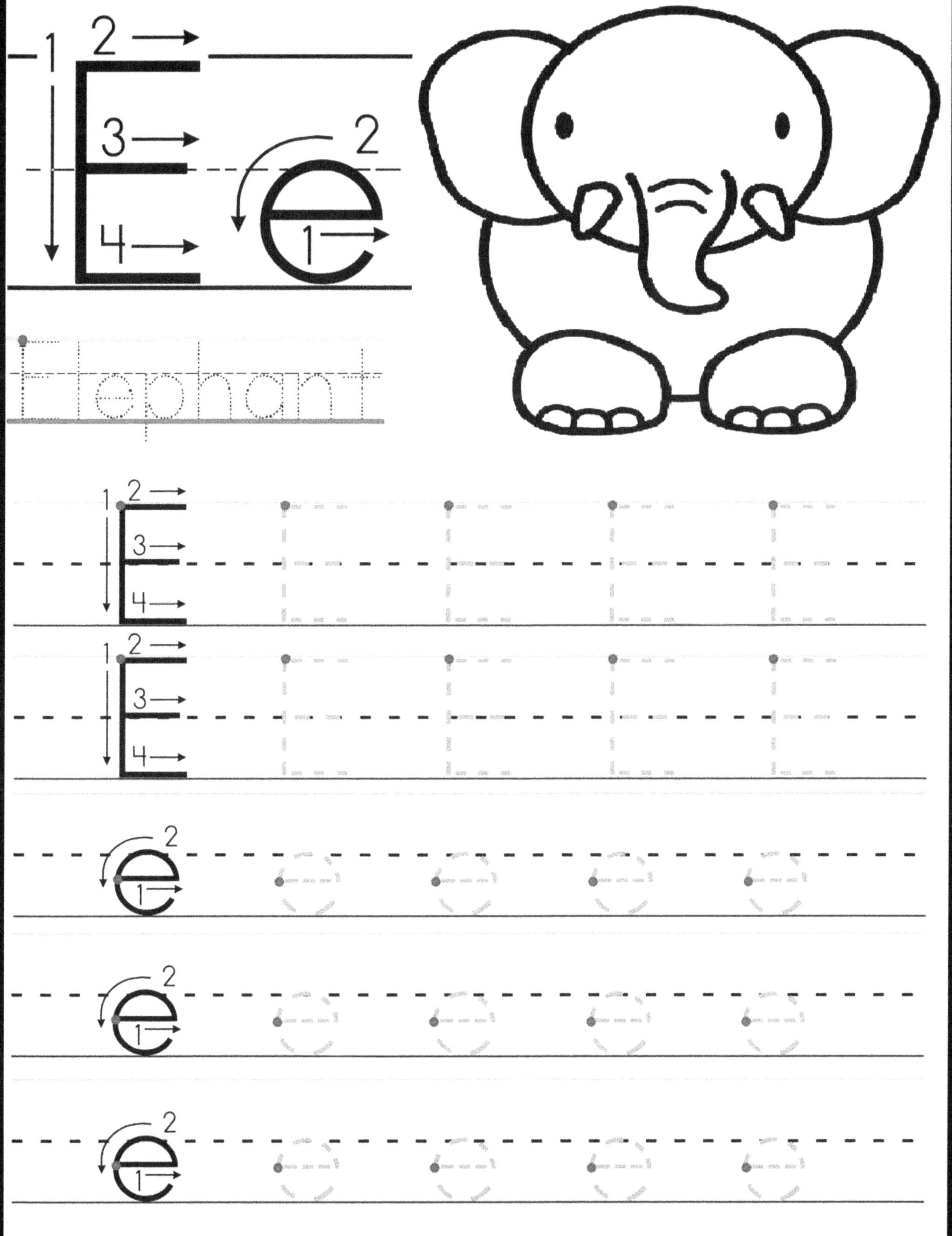

Elephant

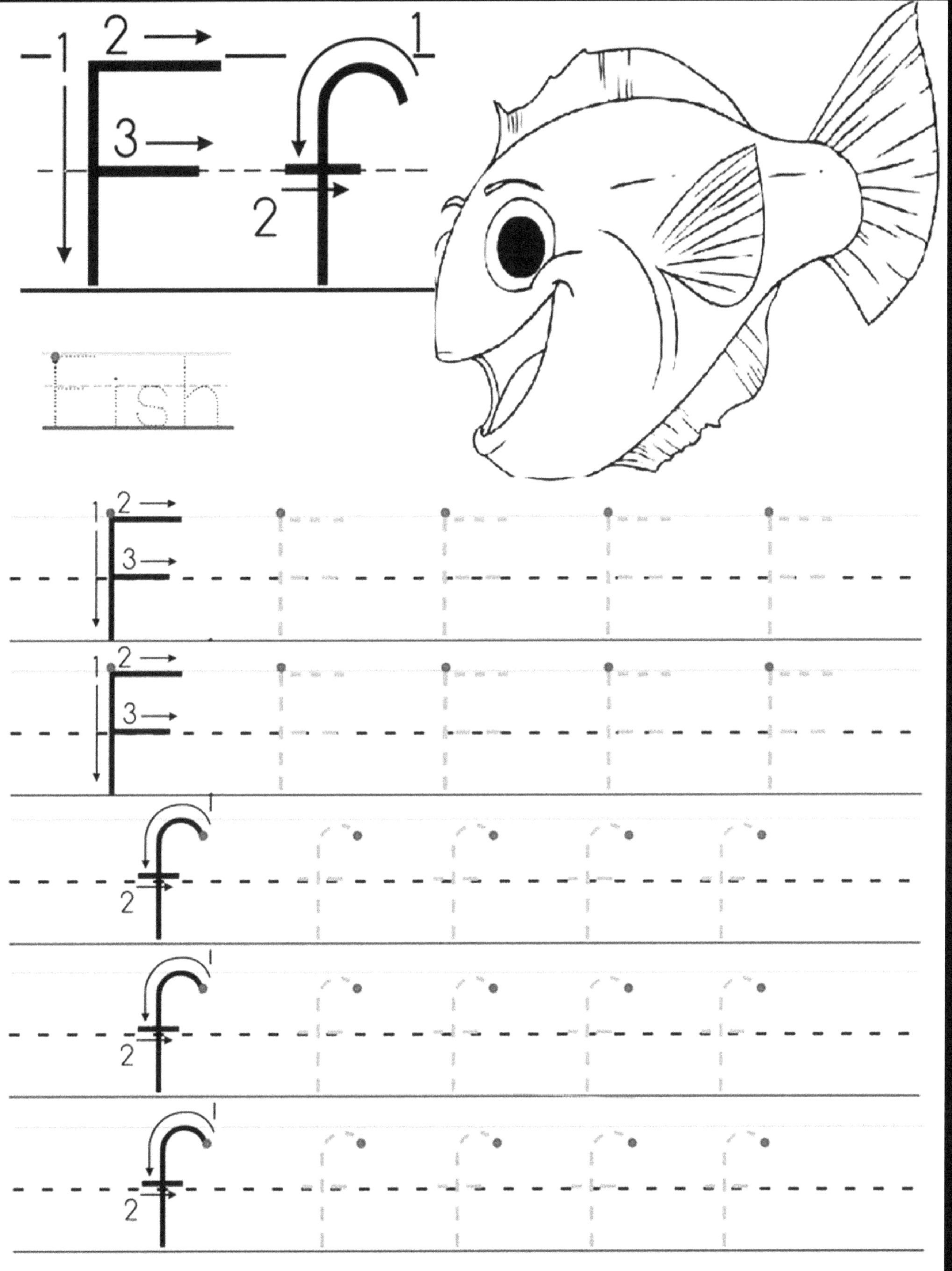
Fish

G g
Gorilla

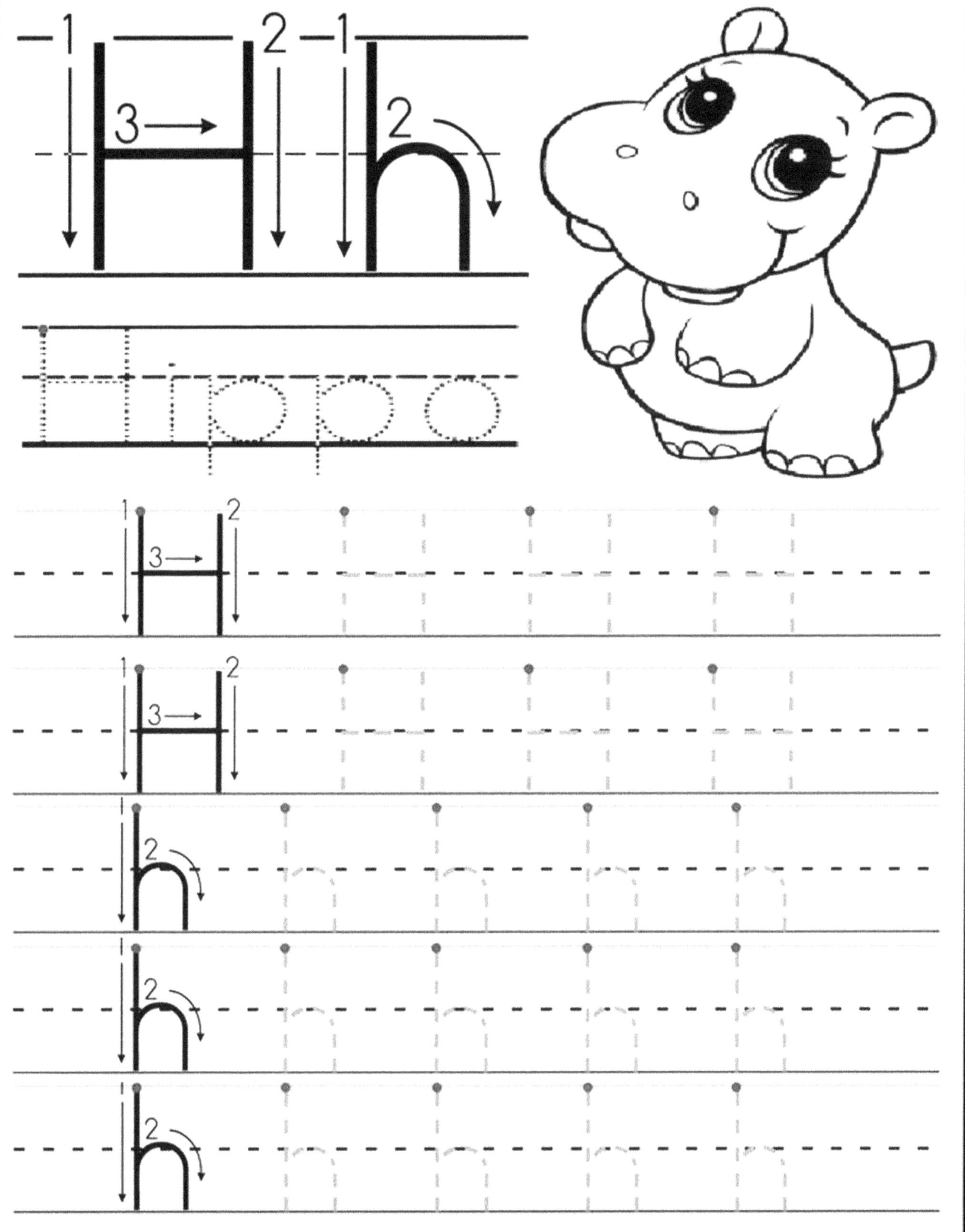

1
2
1
3
2
Hippo
1 2
3
1 2
3
2
2
2

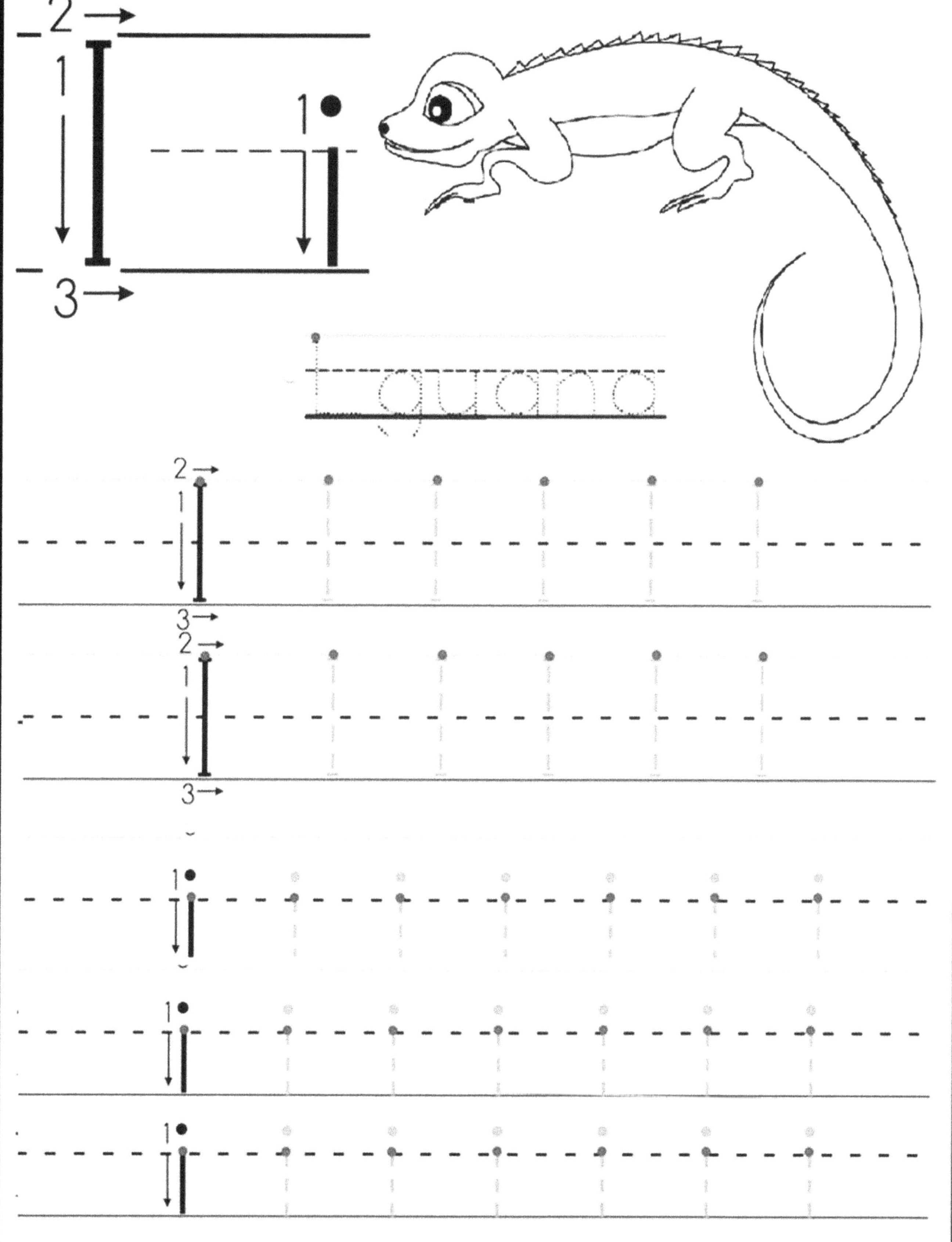

Jellyfish

Kangaroo

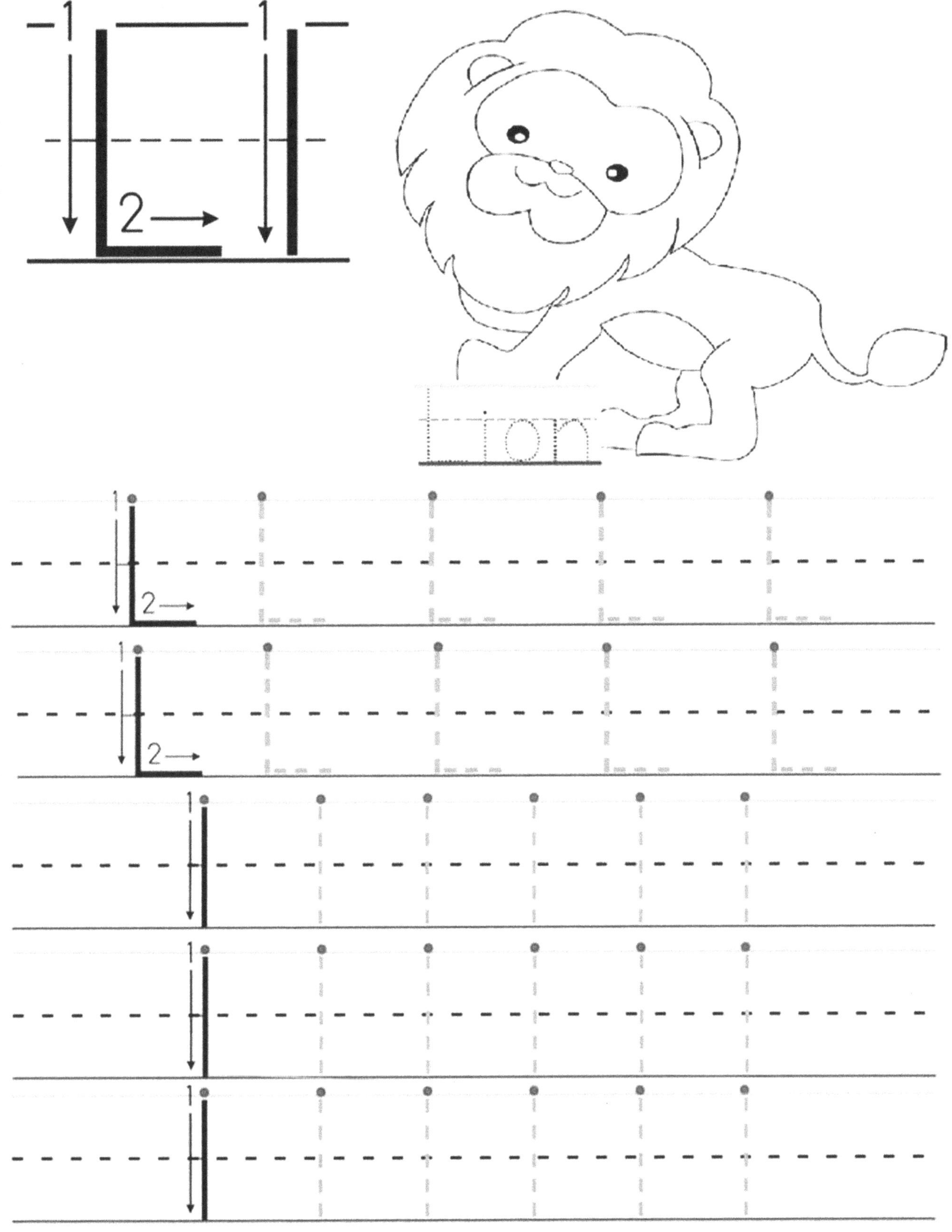
1
2
Lion
1
2
1
2
1
1
1

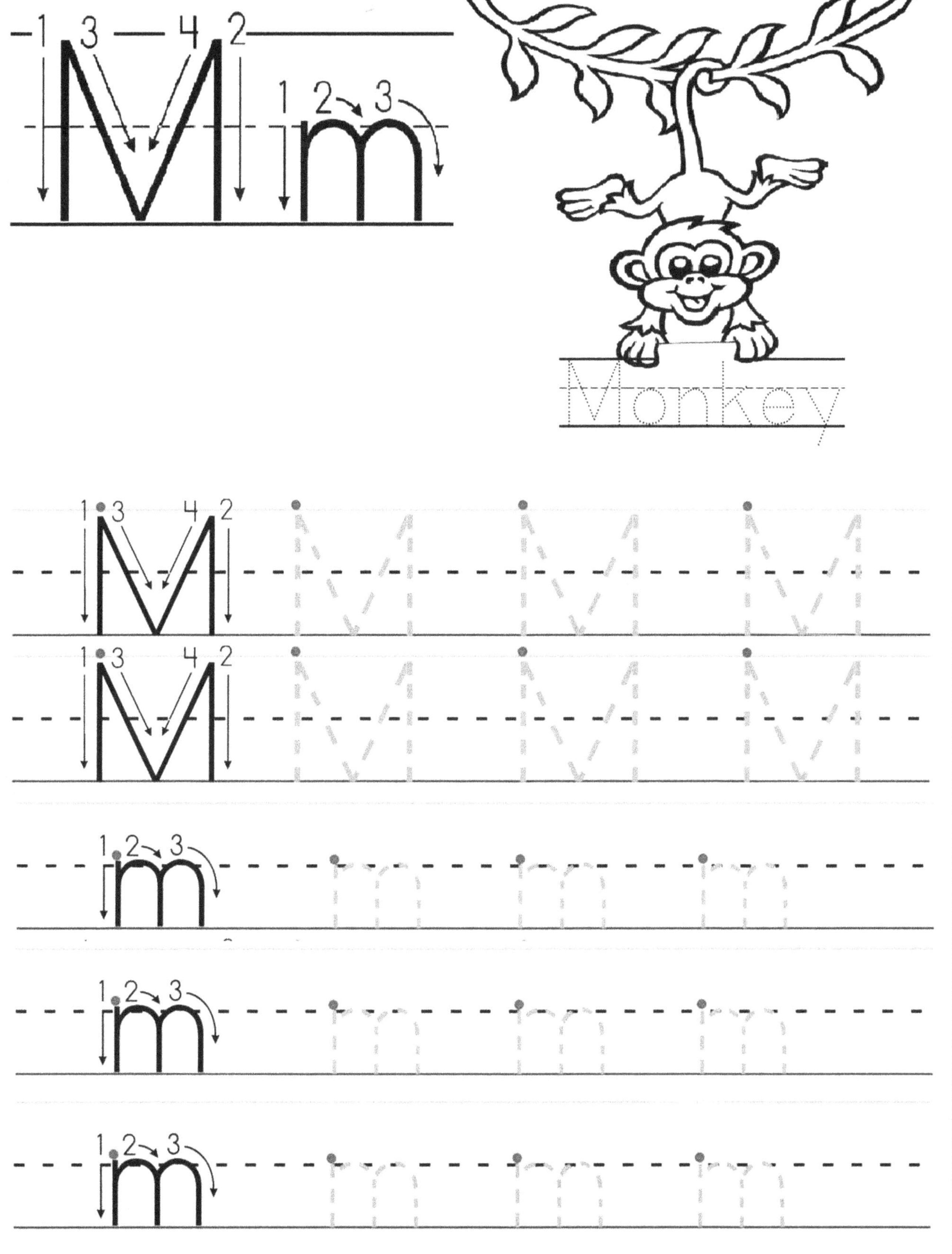

Monkey

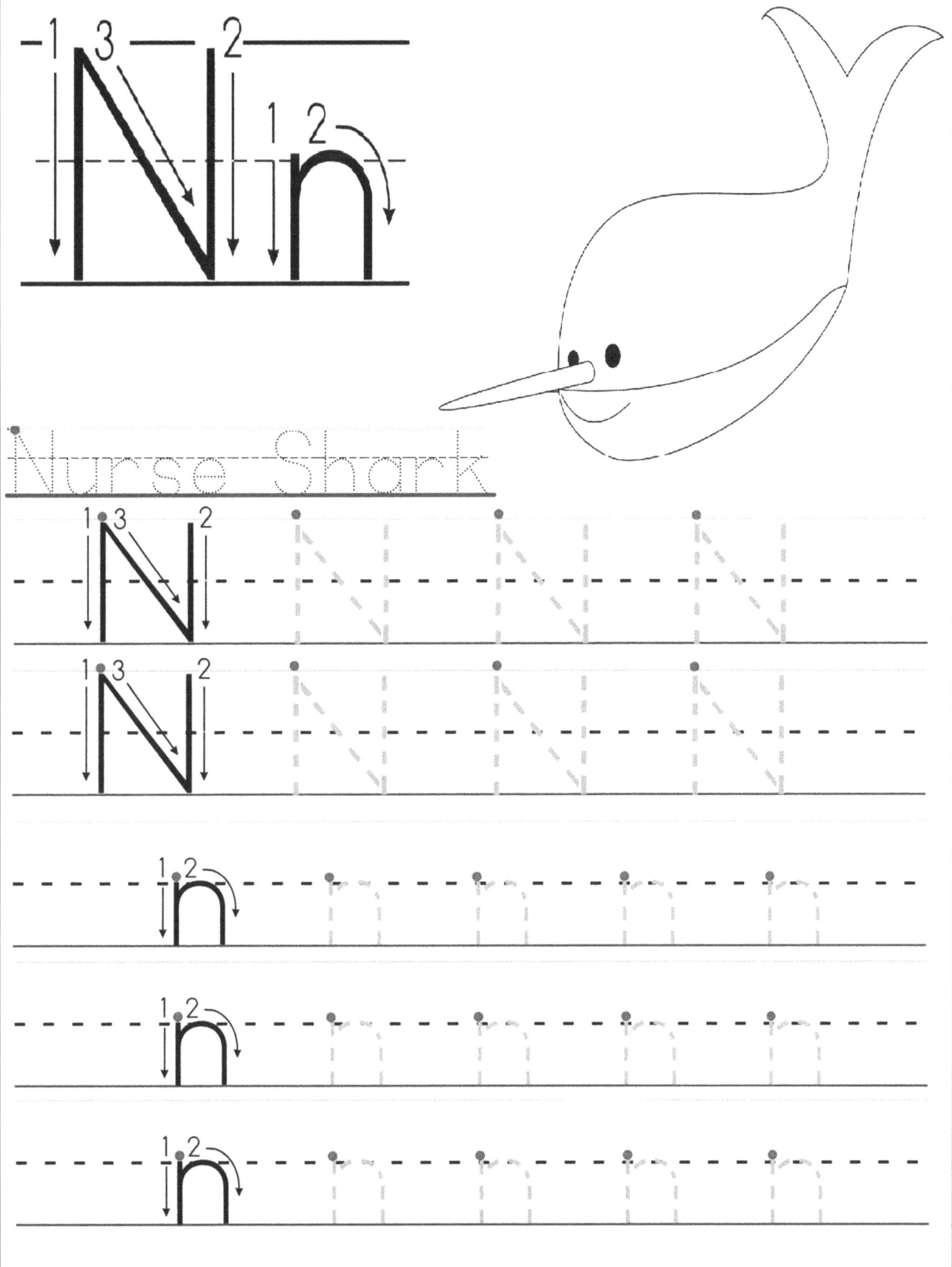
Nurse Shark

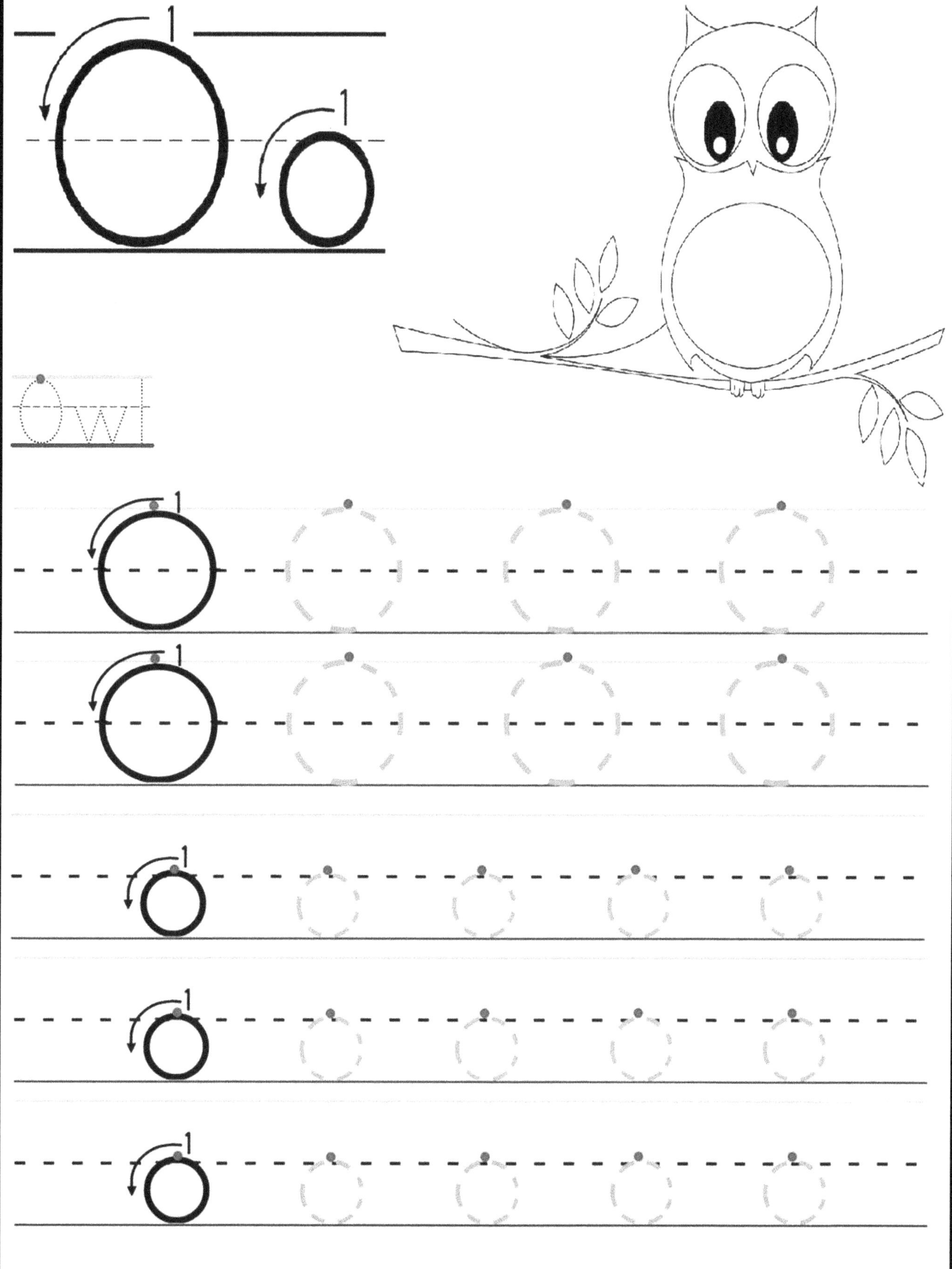
1
1
Owl

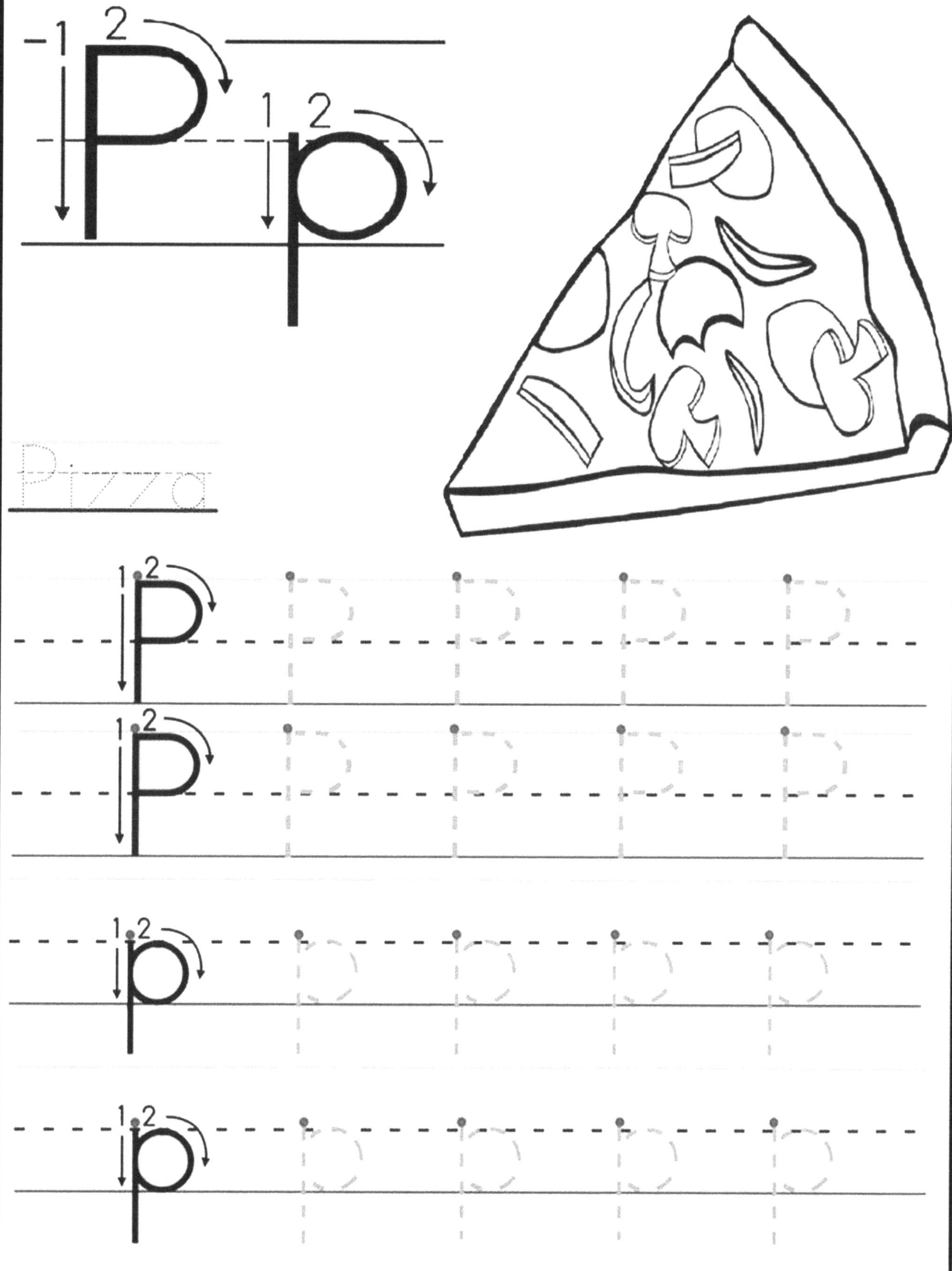

P p

Pizza

Queen

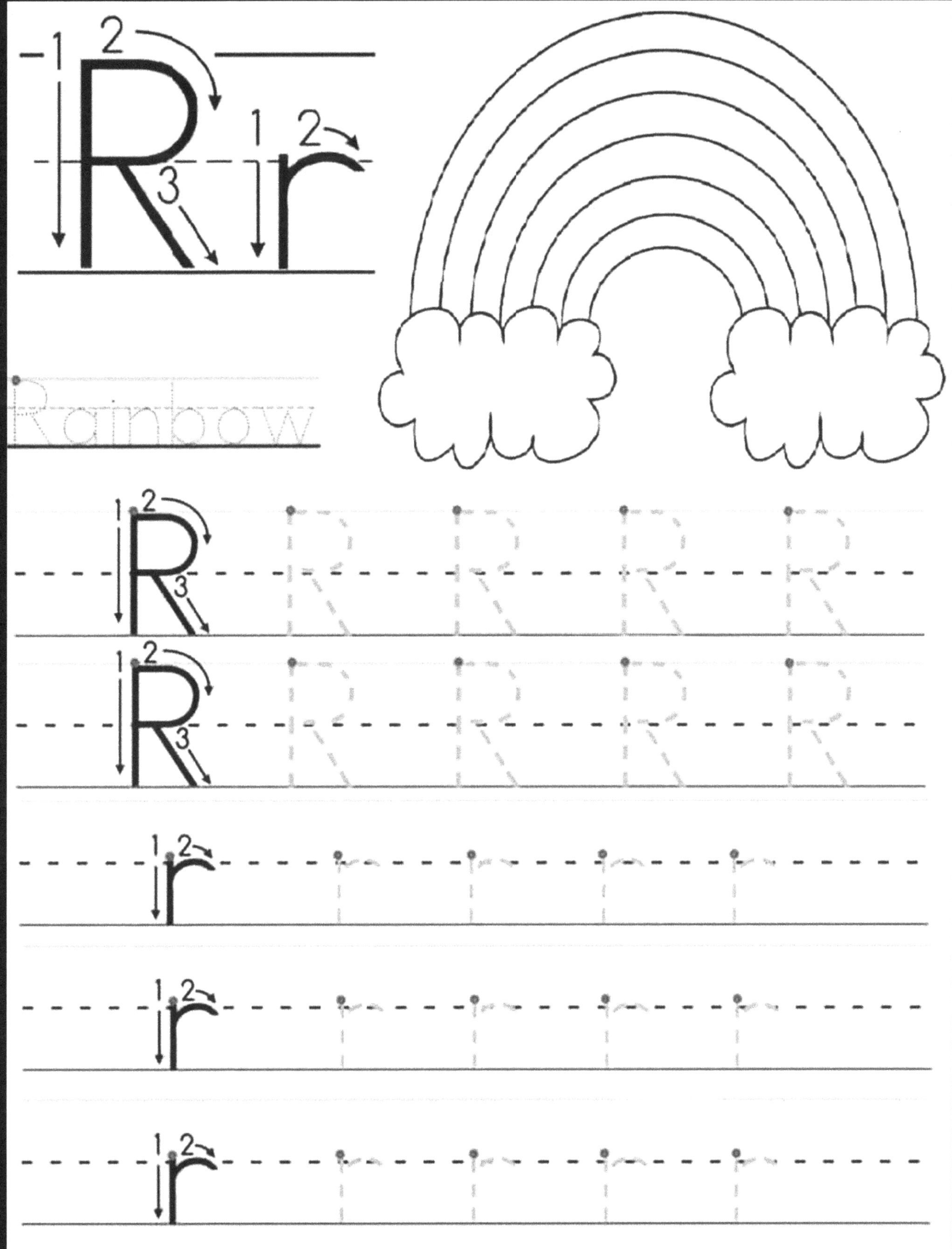
Rainbow

Star

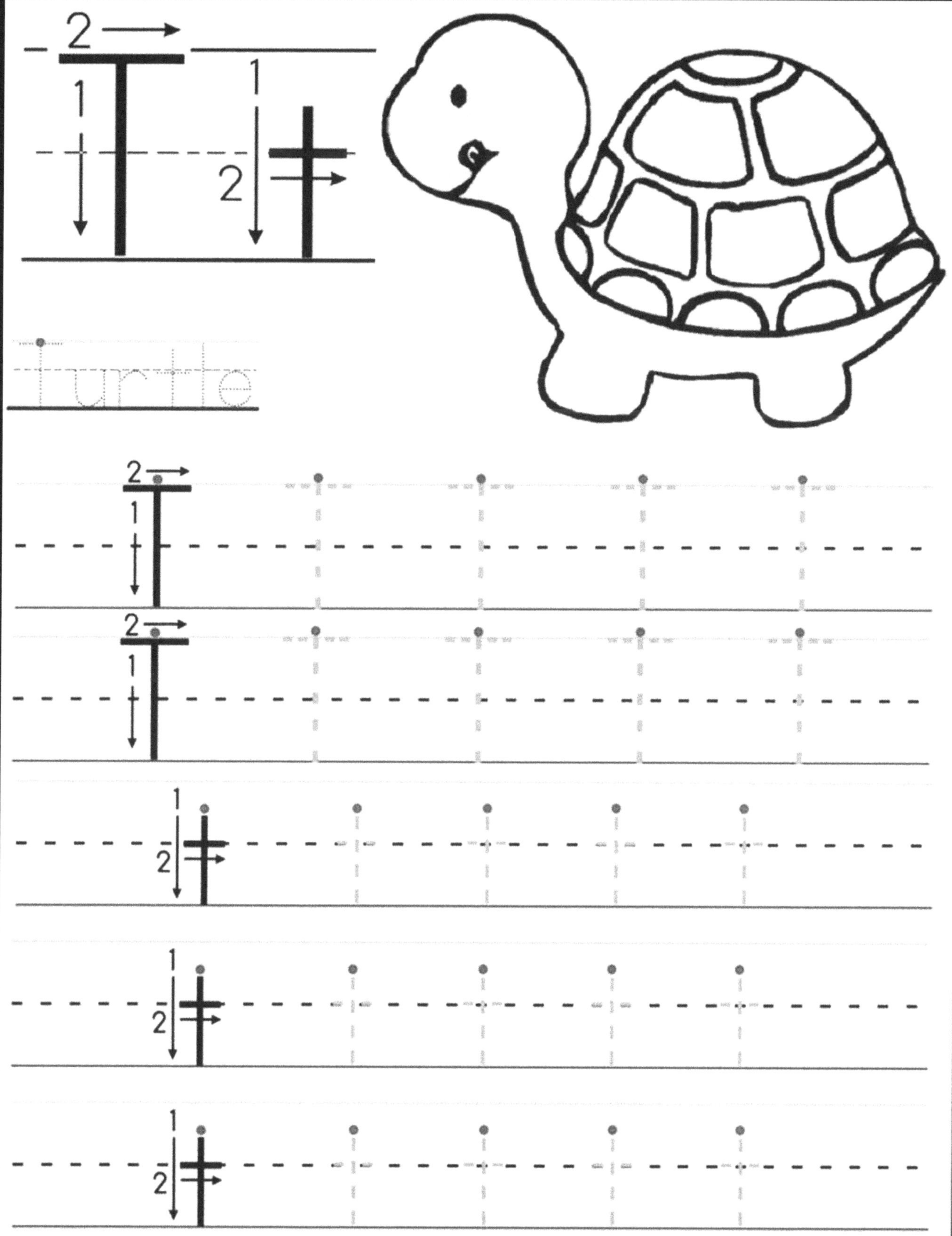

Turtle

U u
umbrella

Worm

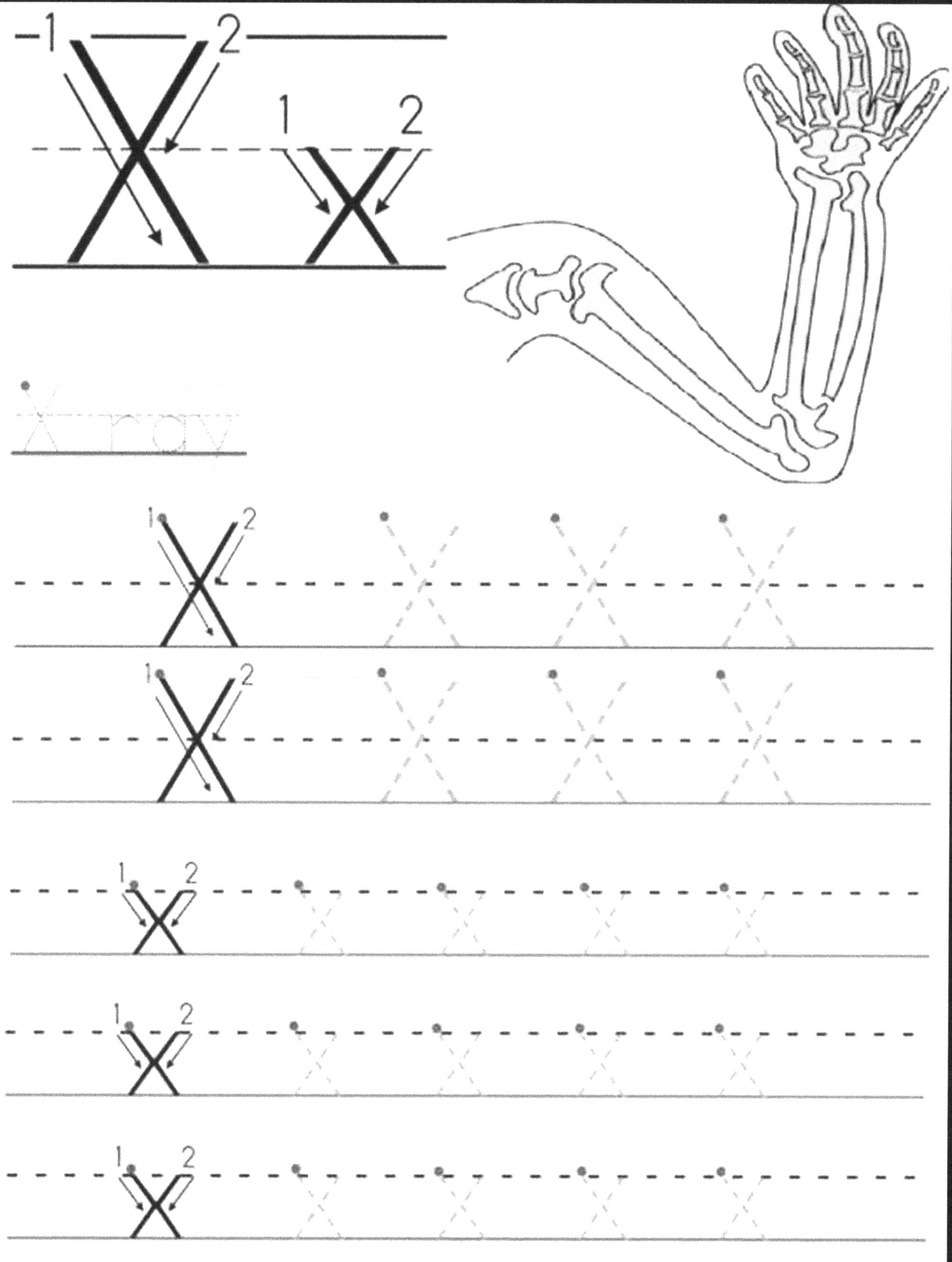

X-ray

Yak

Yak

Zebra

's

ABC Book

A a

B b

C c